THE BLOODLANDS ORACLE

AMORY ABBOTT

REDFeather™
MIND | BODY | SPIRIT
4880 Lower Valley Road, Atglen, PA 19310

Other REDFeather Titles by the Author:
Nightfall Tarot, ISBN 978-0-7643-6623-9

Other REDFeather Titles on Related Subjects:
Guardian Tarot, Beth Seilonen, ISBN 978-0-7643-5386-4
Inner Eye Oracle: A 52-Card Playing Deck for the Modern Age, Steven Bright, ISBN 978-0-7643-6627-7

Library of Congress Control Number: 2024932167

Design by Jack Chappell and Lori Ehrlich
Type set in Loretta/Brandon Grotesque

ISBN: 978-0-7643-6834-9
Printed in China

Published by REDFeather Mind, Body, Spirit
An imprint of Schiffer Publishing, Ltd.
4880 Lower Valley Road
Atglen, PA 19310
Phone: (610) 593-1777; Fax: (610) 593-2002
Email: Info@redfeathermbs.com
Web: www.redfeathermbs.com

For our complete selection of fine books on this and related subjects, please visit our website at www.redfeathermbs.com. You may also write for a free catalog.

REDFeather Mind, Body, Spirit's titles are available at special discounts for bulk purchases for sales promotions or premiums. Special editions, including personalized covers, corporate imprints, and excerpts, can be created in large quantities for special needs. For more information, contact the publisher.

We are always looking for people to write books on new and related subjects. If you have an idea for a book, please contact us at proposals@schifferbooks.com.

Earth has no sorrow
that earth cannot heal.

—JOHN MUIR

INTRODUCTION

Inside you is a wild world: the Bloodlands, an internal landscape where cartomantic and geographic journeys are taken. Winding rivers, sprawling mountains, deep oceans, and vast forests stretch out in all directions, formed by your life, explored, rediscovered, lived in, and died in, many times over. Sometimes you've felt lost, bewildered, thunder-struck, entombed, or at a precipice in your life. Sometimes you've reached an apex, been a refuge, or found a place to rest. Nevertheless, there are old trails to walk again, and new trails to blaze. To explore your internal landscape is to better understand yourself in relation to it, and so *The Bloodlands Oracle* is designed as a guide through the waypoints, landforms, elements, and environmental cataclysms in that dark and ever-changing place. What world will you bring to light along the way?

THE ELEMENTS

Each of the *Bloodlands* cards has a corresponding element that accompanies it, displayed in the top left corner of the card. This element serves as the grounding force of the card, and the experiential subtext of each card's meaning as it relates to the reader. As you read through the cards and interpret them through the spreads, the elements provide an opportunity to position the insight you receive within a deeper context as it relates to fire, water, air, earth, and spirit.

FIRE

Action, passion, power

This element embodies physical movement motivated by the heart, and grounds its cards in the realm of actions.

WATER

Feeling, soul, belief

This element embodies the emotional and spiritual motivations of the heart and grounds its cards in the realm of feelings.

AIR

Thought, intuition, senses

This element embodies the analytical and critical motivations of the mind and grounds its cards in the realm of thoughts.

EARTH

The physical, adornments, health

This element embodies the corporeal and material motivations of the mind and grounds its cards in the physical realm.

SPIRIT

The unknown, external, sacred

This element embodies the etheric influences from outside the body and mind and wields its cards through forces beyond our control.

BLOODLANDS

The following are descriptions of each of the forty-two cards in this deck, along with their corresponding element symbols, modifiers for paired cards, and descriptions for when cards are reversed.

1. THE SAPLING

Growth, coming of age, action

Fed by the earth, water, air, and light, the sapling begins its great journey skyward. This card reveals to us that a long wait is over, and that it is time to grow. Forces have come to your aid, and you are ready to become something greater than you were before. Find the bright opening in the canopy above and strike upward toward it. An opportunity is here, and there is no time to lose!

Growth will be extra speedy if read with The Burn (22).

REVERSED:

Only a fraction of tree seeds ever grow into saplings, and even fewer reach adulthood. In a forest, there is always competition for sunlight, space, nutrients, and time. During periods of growth, we also find ourselves at our most vulnerable. Now is not a time to be reckless. Identify competing forces that could hinder you, because there may be only enough open space for one tree.

2. THE FOOTPATH

Guidance, assistance, trusting in others

The Footpath card offers us a chance to reflect on the paths we follow that have been blazed by those before us. Someone found their way through a wild, unfamiliar place and cleared the way for others to travel. Now is a time to remember those who have helped you get to where you're going, and to express your gratitude. Whose footsteps do you walk in, and who might you eventually leave a path for?

REVERSED:

A footpath is a safe trail through unknown lands but leads to only one place. You will not discover new things if you keep to the trail. Consider that you might need to step off the route, check your bearings, and forge your own path somewhere new.

3. THE DOLMEN

Mystery, faded memory, the limits of knowledge

Dolmens are megalithic "passage tombs" built around six thousand years ago. Burnt human remains have been found inside them, along with ornaments, jewelry, and small tools. The reasons for their construction are still mostly unknown today, but their tunnellike design is believed to represent a threshold to the afterlife. The Dolmen card reminds us that things great and small from our history will fade with time, and that some mysteries will never be fully understood. It's time to let the past remain there, and to give your imagination a passageway to grow through.

REVERSED:

Dolmens are believed to be built for honoring the dead and ensuring their passage into the afterlife. The reversed Dolmen card reminds you there is something lost to your past that needs safe passage into oblivion. What unresolved "dead" issues do you need to let go of for good?

4. DARKNESS

Danger, vigilance, a vulnerable state

When night falls and the world dims, we lose our bearings. Clear paths are lost, pitfalls are unseen, creatures of the night could be all around, and we could be unaware. When light fades from our senses, we are exposed. Unknown things creep up in the dark. The Darkness card finds us at a moment of blindness to possible dangers. It's time to sit tight and wait it out. Find shelter, guard yourself, and wait for daylight to return.

REVERSED:

Darkness in the emotional realm is a place of melancholy, sadness, and fear. What deep wells of feeling can we tap when we travel through the land of darkness in our minds? The emotions you find in dark places are the most powerful. Don't be afraid to seek them out or to let them find you, but know how to wield them, or you may be consumed.

These feelings return from the past if read with the Shadow card (14).

§ 22

5. THE MOONBOW

Revelation, the unorthodox, light in darkness

When moonlight reflects off water droplets in the air, a lunar rainbow, or "moonbow," occurs. It is faint, hard to spot, and an unexpected phenomenon to witness. There is a magical quality to rainbows, and more special are ones that form in darkness. When you let your eyes adjust, you will see that light plays even in the darkest places. Find beauty in your own dim corners.

REVERSED:

Moonbows often appear white because of the low light reflected off the moon. They do not reveal the full spectrum of light that we find in daytime rainbows, and are sometimes too dim to see with the naked eye. What colors are missing from your vision in dim light? The reversed Moonbow reminds us that when we lack sufficient light in our lives, we cannot see all the colors of possibility.

Some patience is needed if read with the Darkness card (4).

6. THE DISTANT RANGE

Foresight, adventure, long-term goals

The towering range in the distance, soft and hazy, invites us to set out on a journey to discover what lies beyond. The Distant Range card represents a look into our future, asking us to perceive what lies ahead, and to commit to long-term goals. What awaits you in the distant vision of your life? What point on the horizon can you move toward?

REVERSED:

The range you see in the distance may be compelling, but what takes place in the land between here and there? Reversed, the Distant Range card asks us to remember what lies in the foreground that we overlook, when transfixed on distant hopes. What adventures, treacherous or otherwise, await only a few steps away?

7. THE CASCADE

Momentum, easing of tension, windfall

A newly formed stream meanders its way lazily to the steep edge of a ravine, where the ground drops sharply to a pool far below. At the ledge, patiently winding waters suddenly straighten and rush down the rocks, gifted by gravity and a clear path down. This card finds you at the end of a period of slow but deliberate movement, ready to cut loose. Let this new opportunity for acceleration hasten you toward a goal. Let go and make things happen; gravity is on your side.

This opportunity may be bigger than you think if read with The Falls (26).

REVERSED:

Cascades are often the product of an overflowed tributary. This release of tension is natural and necessary but is often a symptom of greater problems upstream. Have you overfilled a reservoir in your life? Before you find methods to ease the pressure, consider identifying what excessive things flooded you in the first place.

8. THE OLD BRIDGE

Connection, friendship, long-term commitments

The Old Bridge card represents the long-standing connection between two people. An alliance was made long ago and still stands to this day. Whether the bridge between you two is still in use or has fallen into antiquity, remember that it still exists, as a real pathway or only symbolically. It's time to reach out to an old friend.

Rekindle an old collaboration if read with The Confluence (25).

REVERSED:

Abandoned to time, the oldest bridges are more of a symbol of old relationships rather than a functional necessity. You may have found more efficient routes over the river or decided that it was better to keep to your own side. Are you still accessible to someone or something that is no longer serving your interests? Perhaps it's time to burn that bridge, for your own well-being.

9. THE CLOUDVEIL

Patience, perseverance, hidden truths, saving the best for last

A "cloudveil" is the covering of lenticular clouds over the top of a mountain, shrouding its peak from view. While we know the summit is there, it is obscured from our immediate vision. What heights do we not yet see clearly in our lives? What results remain a mystery? The Cloudveil card reminds us that the rewards of our endeavors may not be apparent, but they are surely awaiting us, and we must continue on nevertheless until they are revealed.

REVERSED:

The cloudveil hides not only peaks, but truths as well. There are truths within us that we keep hidden from the ones we care about, but in doing so, we do not share the greatest and most authentic parts of ourselves. What secrets do you keep behind the clouds that need to be uncovered?

Expect those secrets to be dangerous if read with The Solitary Peak (18).

10. THE MEADOW

Personal space, relaxation, pleasure

Forming an opening deep inside the busy and dark canopy, a meadow is bathed in light. Host to wildflowers, soft grass, and the most delicate of forest creatures, the Meadow card represents a time of calmness and personal ease in your life. It's time to breathe deeply, let your body relax, and watch the dragonflies dance around you.

REVERSED:

A meadow is a gathering place for many beings, sought out through the dark and dangerous forest. A well-kept secret, it is where magic lives and there is room to frolic. Reversed, the Meadow card calls to you to seek out a community of others to relax and play with. A reading group, a club, a movement. It's time to find your people.

11. THE LIGHTNING STRIKE

Dramatic change, destruction and renewal

The Lightning Strike card represents a sudden and dramatic force of change. The power of a single bolt may topple an entire forest, but a forest relies on cataclysmic events like these for ecological succession. The smoldering ashes of destruction nourish the ground, and eventually life returns; a new forest grows, stronger and healthier than the last. Life can always change in a flash.

REVERSED:

Lightning is the byproduct of two great opposing forces equalizing each other. Too much energy is generated and must be released, often violently. Are you building tension where it need not be?

12. THE BURNT SNAG

Endurance, transcendence, sacrifice

A burnt snag is the remnant trunk of a tree taken by fire. Its original life is gone, but the tree is still very much alive in new ways. It is a home to nesting birds and small mammals, its ashes enrich the soil around it, and even the loss of its crown lets more light into the forest for young saplings to grow. This card asks us to see the new ways we can find meaning and thrive in the wake of great loss or change.

Think of what experience you might offer others if read with The Nurse Log (40).

REVERSED:

The benefits of a snag are often overlooked within a forest teeming with green life. We tend to distract ourselves from the "lost" things in our life, to avoid facing the way they live on in the back of our hearts. A snag in your life needs attention.

△

13. THE CAVERN

Introspection, things hidden, temperance

Caverns are ancient underground waterways carved over thousands if not millions of years. These paths into and through the earth are places of safety and retreat, not only to humans but to animals seeking refuge, winter hibernation, and quiet time. The Cavern card reveals a need to seek solitude, to look within, to spend time with the internal self. What answers lie within, away from the influence of others?

Consider an introspective solo retreat if read with The High Fells (16).

REVERSED:

Caverns are not only places of solitude, but places of hiding. When the Cavern card is reversed, it asks us: What people or situations send you into hiding? What is something you have avoided facing? It may be time to leave the cave and step into the light.

14. SHADOW

Mindfulness, affect, thoughtfulness

Our shadow is a distorted version of ourselves, the intrusive shape of us that is cast across our surroundings and across others. Our movements, actions, and body language follow us in an intangible form, shading anything it touches. When we are exposed in the light, our shadows fall. It follows our steps, mimics us, exposes our every move. The Shadow card asks us to understand that what we do in our lives leaves a trace across other things. The light of truth is shining on you; it's time to tread carefully, and mindfully.

REVERSED:

Our shadow is our dark twin, the side of us that we do not like yet cannot escape. Our inner thoughts, secrets, and regrets live as our shadow, taking every step we do, following us wherever we go. You're stuck with them, like it or not. Reversed, the Shadow card asks you to stop running from it, and to accept that it is and will always be a part of you. Embrace your shortcomings and invite them to learn from the person you are now.

15. THE ALPINE LAKE

Reprieve, a rest after difficult work, tranquility

The climb is hard to reach the lake in the mountains, but there is no way to reach a more serene place. The cleanest water in the world is fed by Alpine glaciers; it pools in lakes high above the timberline and is an oasis for weary travelers. The Alpine Lake card reassures us that with great effort comes great reward; whether the result is great wealth, peaceful rest, or a simple drink of fresh water, the calm, clean lake above the trees is well worth the journey.

Expect a long period of rest if read with The Glacier (39).

REVERSED:

Glacier-fed lakes are the water towers of continents, holding a reserve of water that nourishes all that it passes as it rushes down in mountain streams. This time-release resource may not come as quickly as needed in some areas. What needs in your life may require more than can be given?

▽

16. THE HIGH FELLS

Keeping secrets, risk, banishment

On a treacherous path up a steep rock face, you reach the High Fells, where secrets are kept far from even the most adventurous explorers. Deep inside the cliff, ancient knowledge is hidden away, but for what purpose? It can only be assumed that whatever was put there was not meant to be known about, and difficult to reconcile. The High Fells card reminds us that no matter how deeply buried, old wounds still exist if not brought to light to heal. It's time to free something locked deep inside.

Something is worth letting go of through ceremony if read with The Tomb (20).

REVERSED:

What lies hidden away may be dangerous knowledge, but it was put there by people with great effort. Secrets are being kept from you by someone who'd rather not revisit the past. What could those secrets be?

17. THE MOUNTAIN PASS

Fortune, a needed break, skillful planning

The Mountain Pass card represents a welcomed easing in the demands of life. Trails over a mountain pass often cross the lowest "gap" between two peaks, maximizing efficiency and requiring the least amount of effort to cross a mountain range without going around. What is the shortest route you can take to reach a goal you've set? Best you find it and gift it to yourself.

REVERSED:

The pass over a mountain will not meander, not explore, not challenge you more than necessary. Accomplishment is almost guaranteed, but growth is not. What valuable experience might you be avoiding for the sake of comfort?

18. THE SOLITARY PEAK

Independence, self-confidence, grandiosity

This card reveals the power of a lone mountain peak, standing tall, ruling over its domain as a symbol of independent spirit. We all strive to be strong and self-sufficient, and we all have it within us to be a solitary peak in many aspects of our life. Now is a good time to honor your efforts, celebrate your achievements, and bask in your own majesty.

REVERSED:

While standing tall and independent, a solitary peak can also be characterized by loneliness, isolation, and even volatility—solitary peaks are often active volcanoes, building pressure that must be released at times. What pressures could be growing by isolating yourself from others?

Look into your past for answers if read with The Caldera (38).

19. TWILIGHT

A winding down, endings, perseverance

The sun has set, yet darkness has not fallen. The last rays of light beyond the horizon still illuminate the sky. This is a time of ending, but not quite the end. The Twilight card reminds us that there is still time left to accomplish the things we set out to do, even if it seems that it is too late. Push on; there is still time to complete something, still time to heal, still time to forgive, still time to make things right.

This may be your last chance if read with the Darkness card (4).

REVERSED:

As the day fades, things become obscured in the dimming light. We lose focus, lose our sense of surroundings or sense of direction. It is a time of transition from the external to the internal. When the Twilight card is reversed, it is time to close your eyes, forget how things look on the surface, and let your other senses guide you.

20. THE TOMB

Death, things buried, past selves or events

The Tomb card represents what has been buried, or something that we thought was buried that has come back into our lives. To be placed in a tomb is to honor that which has passed on beyond the material. It is the memorial of a being or a way of being that is no longer necessary. The death of an old self, of an old relationship, of old habits or beliefs. The Tomb card is a call to let something go, but in reverence.

REVERSED:

To bury something can be an attempt to hide the past from our present. What difficult things in your life have been hidden away, sealed within a dark crypt? What challenges have you avoided dealing with? Who or what from your past still haunts you?

21. THE CROWN FIRE

Devastation, total collapse, starting over

A wildfire burns in different intensities, the crown fire being the most destructive, since the flames will destroy the top "crown" of trees. When this happens, the tree will certainly die, since it cannot continue to grow and the fire has reached a height that eradicates all other plants and animals living in and around the tree. New seeds and animals must eventually migrate back from other forests in order for it to regrow, and with time it will. This card comes at a time of great endings, where the only way to recover may be with help from the outside.

REVERSED:

Most tree species survive lower-intensity ground fires due to their thick bark. Crown fires occur more rarely, when the conditions in the forest are more extreme. What conditions in you might be getting too extreme to recover from?

22. THE BURN

Healing trauma, recovery, rejuvenation

The forest after a wildfire can be an apocalyptic scene. Blackened snags, toppled trunks, ashen ground devoid of life. What lies under the charred soil, however, are the seeds of the next great forest, and the heat of the fire has just cracked them open. When we experience trauma, it may be impossible at the time to see our future growth and well-being, yet it is there, quietly sprouting. The Burn card reminds us that healing is on its way, whether you feel it or not.

REVERSED:

When a forest burns down, what comes next will not be the same. It will not grow back the way it was. New species of animals, trees, and plants arrive from other regions, on the back of winds and in the stomachs of birds. The new life will be unfamiliar. Embrace the mystery of what will come next.

Expect that the change will be extreme if read with The Crown Fire (21).

23. HEADWATERS

Youth, innocence, excitement for new things, early stages

The Headwaters card reminds us that all things start small, but in that smallness is the potential for all things. Even the mightiest river begins as a trickling spring in the mountains. Trust that no matter how small an idea or plan in your life may be, it has the potential to become something great. It's time to focus on the small beginnings of something new in your life.

Look for support from a friend or partner if read with The Sapling (1), or consider the ways your social connections may bolster this small start in the future if read with The Confluence (25).

REVERSED:

Something has grown too big, gotten out of control. Trace back to the early stages of it, in order to remember when the river of it was once a playful brook leading out of the forest.

24. THE RIVER

Direction, momentum, going with the flow

A river follows the path of least resistance, carving its way slowly over eons through rock and earth, carrying all that joins it to its end. It grows the more it is fed, and is harnessed for its power. It is a home to fish and other animals, it feeds the plants along its bank and the fields it divides, and its surface is traveled upon great distances, connecting worlds. Be reassured; this card finds you in a state of consistent movement toward your goals, carrying you effortlessly where you desire.

Consider a project with a friend or partner if read with The Confluence (25).

REVERSED:

A river gently carries all that surrender to its direction, but it can be a destructive force when it meets resistance. Working against it is futile, exhausting, and dangerous. What are you resisting?

▽

25. THE CONFLUENCE

Collaboration, unity, cooperation

Two great rivers meet at a confluence. They become one entity, entwined and inseparable, and together they double their strength and momentum. This card may represent new partnerships—friends, lovers, colleagues—who join their strength with yours in order to achieve a greater purpose. It's time to acknowledge the person at your side and give thanks to each other.

REVERSED:

A confluence is not always the meeting of equals. One river can often be a tributary of another, feeding the larger one on its original path. Be careful to not lose yourself in the flow of another, but strive to work together toward one direction. Whom might you be feeding, and who may be feeding you?

Slow yourself down in this collaboration if read with The Cascade (7).

26. THE FALLS

Completion, release, a new phase

The Falls card finds us in a time of free-falling. We might not know what lies at the bottom of the drop, or where we will flow onto next, but this moment is about letting go. The widening river of our life has reached a precipice, and we now tumble over the edge toward the next stage of our journey. Trust that the river will continue toward the ocean, but expect a splash before it calms down.

Expect the unexpected if read with The Chasm (36).

REVERSED:

A waterfall finds the most efficient way to the bottom of a cliff, but its speed is granted at the risk of dashing whatever falls with it upon the rocks below. You're impatient about something right now. Don't rush. Try to find a safer way down the hillside.

27. THE ISLAND

Independence, self-reliance, wholeness

An island contains a fully functioning ecosystem. No matter the size, the life it holds is self-sustaining; a complete circle. As an individual, an island can depend on itself, and only under extreme circumstances will it require external aid. The Island card asks you to trust in yourself, to know that you are enough. The opportunity has come to believe in yourself, and your abilities. Everything you need is within you.

REVERSED:

Islands are separated from larger landforms, and while they are self-sufficient, their isolation restricts their ability to grow and change. Not much diversity is found on small islands, and some are difficult to reach. All solitude comes at the cost of community. Have you pushed yourself away from important connections? It's time to renew lost relationships.

Steer clear of old, toxic relationships if read with The Solitary Peak (18), or reach out to a past aquaintance if read with The Old Bridge (8).

28. ANTHELION

An omen, portent of change, foreshadowing

Meaning "opposite the sun," *anthelion* is a light phenomenon that creates faint spots along sunbows and rainbows and may be crossed by a pair of diffused arcs of light. Ancient northern traditions believed that these spots were two wolves chasing the sun and moon across the sky. It foreshadowed a day the wolves would finally catch up and devour them, plunging the world into darkness. Great change is on its way. Good or bad, this is your warning.

This destructive change will create unexpected blessings if paired with The Moonbow (5).

REVERSED:

Look at the shadow of your head on a sunny day, and you will likely see a faint ring of light around it. The darkness we see that opposes the sun is always encircled by more intense brightness. You are focusing on the dark places in yourself right now—it's time to recognize your brightest self at the edges of the shadow.

29. THE STONE CIRCLE

Communion, connection, higher understanding

The oldest human-made structures on the planet are stone circles. Cultures from around the world have used stone circles across millennia as places of gathering and worship. Often oriented geographically toward celestial cycles, these circles are believed to harness the power of the universe, bringing those who enter the circle closer together, and connecting them with a greater conscience. This card urges you to seek out the counsel of your friends, and to share collective wisdom in the ancient tradition.

REVERSED:

The council circle creates space for a community of minds, brought together with a greater purpose. When reversed, this card finds you outside the circle, left to your own devices. When a circle cannot be formed, how will you rely on your own experience as a teacher? Look inside; there is another circle within you. Ask it what you need.

30. THE ERRATIC

The unexpected, interruption, imposition

A boulder deposited by glacial movement in an unexpected location is called an erratic. Imagine a large mass of rock at rest in an empty field; an unavoidable and worrying form in an otherwise calm environment. The Erratic card reveals that something unexpected has found its way into the familiar, and while it may be something that has always been there, it needs to be acknowledged.

REVERSED:

An erratic is carried by forces beyond its control to a place it is not suited for. We are often forced into situations or places that we do not want to be. While we may not have a choice in our placement, we do have the opportunity to find ways of fitting in. How are you resisting the place you have found yourself?

31. THE GATEWAY

New opportunities, expansion, crossing a threshold

The Gateway card comes to us at a time of transition. A gateway signifies an entrance, a mile marker, the next stage of a process. Symbolically, it is a learning experience, a leveling up, the boundary between the past and the future. You are about to cross into a new way of being. Prepare yourself.

REVERSED:

As you cross the thresholds of understanding, remember that you can seldom go back. The greatest choices often come at a price, and that is that you may never return to where you were before. Think twice about a big decision. It may cost more than you can bear to lose.

Reconsider old options if read with The Crossroads (34) card, or seek professional advice if read with The Footpath (2).

32. ERUPTION

Energy release, equilibrium, restoration

Not only is the profound release of energy in an eruption a volcano's means of restoring order to the planet's interior, but the nitrogen-rich ash that falls from the blast is a natural fertilizer for plant life, greatly benefiting the ecosystem around its base. For us, finding constructive ways of releasing pent-up energy has a restorative effect on our emotional well-being and enriches the relationships we have with those around us. It's time to find a healthy way to unwind.

Seek the wisdom of your elders if read with The Caldera (38).

REVERSED:

When enough pressure builds under the earth, gases mix with viscous lava and explode upward in a frothy cloud of ash and debris. This mixture of two volatile elements will create an intense energy that cannot be contained. Reversed, the Eruption card reminds us that we all have triggers that set us off. It's time to identify yours and reexamine your boundaries.

33. THE SCREE

Exposure, vulnerability, unexpected benefits

Massive piles of rock rubble form when the side of a mountain breaks free and tumbles to the bottom of the slope below. Known as scree, these shattered mounds appear at first to be desolate areas. A closer look reveals that in the spaces between the boulders, Alpine animals build their homes together in large communal networks of tunnels and nests, sheltered from predators and inclement weather. What safe systems are formed in the wake of vulnerable situations? Find friendships within the wreckage.

REVERSED:

Scree can be the byproduct of an unstable ecosystem. A lack of adequate hydration and wildfires can cause soil on a mountainside to loosen and crumble, sometimes suddenly. You may be experiencing a shortage of something crucial to your stability. Time to take inventory of your ecosystem and ask for what you need.

34. CROSSROADS

Facing difficult choices, new opportunities, networking

When you come to an intersection of pathways, you may know where you need to go, or the best way forward may be unclear. When we encounter new opportunities, it can be hard to choose a direction confidently. You may meet others traveling in different directions at an intersection who can tell you where they've been, and where they're going. What choices lie before you, and whose wisdom can you seek to help you decide?

REVERSED:

Having too many choices can be a distraction from what is necessary. A crossroads can sometimes sidetrack you when an overpass would have helped you stay focused. What fantasies are keeping you from the clear way forward?

35. RADIANCE

Exposure, recognition, truth

Everything is bathed in light at the moment. Whether you find warmth, joy, revelation, or explanation, now is a time that everything is clear. Revel in the brilliance of the world, seek out what has been hidden, and trust the honest path. Let the truth be your guide. If you need answers; it's time to ask for them.

REVERSED:

In the brilliant light of the sun, we cast the sharpest shadow. Nothing in us is hidden, and so it is an opportunity to practice being the person you see yourself as. Look inside and find the person in you that needs light. What have you been holding back? It's time to show your hand, to let the world know exactly who you are.

If read with the Shadow card (14), you might not like what comes out. It's your responsibility to own it regardless.

36. THE CHASM

Fear of the unknown, emptiness, a time of loss

The Chasm card reveals a deep place in us that we are unfamiliar with. Toss a stone in and you may never hear it hit the bottom. It is a void that things fall into and are lost, seemingly forever. There is no way to know what lies beyond what we can see, yet we are compelled to peer over the edge, to understand the depths within us all and remember what was lost. Keep your curiosity alive but mind the gap.

REVERSED:

A chasm, much like a black hole, only consumes, never giving in return. Sometimes in the struggle to know ourselves better, we only take, and we forget that others need your gifts in return. What energy could you reciprocate to those peering over your edges?

37. THE TIMBERLINE

Boundaries, limitations, borders

The highest point on a mountain where trees are still able to grow is called the timberline. This edge of wilderness gives way to another kind of wilderness: one of low shrubs, barren rock, snow, and ice. The Timberline card presents us with a boundary—literal or figurative—in our lives that we cannot thrive on the other side of. You are called to identify a personal limit and find safe ways to live within it.

REVERSED:

Every edge is a marginal space, a place where transition occurs. The space between the forest and the bare slope is constantly undergoing transformation. The push and pull of being one thing and another always requires liminal space. Find ways to stretch your boundaries, to challenge your own limitations. Where can your life expand?

38. THE CALDERA

Incarnation, healing old wounds, purification

In the vent of an ancient volcano, soil collapses slowly into the hole, creating a circular crater. In some rare cases, groundwater will fill the depression, forming a small lake inside the cone. Filtered through volcanic rock, the water is vibrant and deep blue and considered sacred in cultures around the world. The Caldera card asks us to find an old wound in our lives and transform it into a sacred site. What will you fill with the deepest blue?

REVERSED:

Calderas are classified in a dangerous category of volcanoes, if still active. A mass of lava sits just below the crater, building a concentrated pressure in a small space. What might be sitting below your calm cool surface, ready to erupt?

▽

39. THE GLACIER

Patience, resilience, modesty

Glaciers are nature's water towers. They hold an immense amount of liquid and release it slowly in warm months, regulating the health of the entire ecosystem below. Even in droughts, glaciers will keep the land and its inhabitants alive with clear, reliable meltwater. The Glacier card reminds us to trust in our hidden resources, and to develop a reliable consistency in how we replenish ourselves. It may be time to follow a healthy new routine.

REVERSED:

Glaciers sit at the top, literally, of a fragile ecosystem. When glaciers melt too quickly from rising air temperatures, they are unable to regain their mass over winter. When meltwater runs out, every part of the system below it is disrupted. Something in your life is taking too much from you, and it's affecting all the other parts of your life that rely on your resiliency. Rein in your output.

40. THE NURSE LOG

Legacy, inheritance, humility

When a dead tree finally falls, it begins to decompose in place, releasing its last nutrients back into the ground. Its body becomes a rich soil for other seeds to take root, as the ridge of this "nurse log" becomes an ecosystem of its own. Supporting the growth of numerous plants and other tree species over hundreds of years, the Nurse Log asks us this: What legacy will we leave behind once we die? How will you lay the foundation for others to grow from your wisdom and successes? How do you want to be remembered?

Children or mentorship may be the focus if read with The Sapling (1).

REVERSED:

Strong trees grow from the soil of a nurse log. Their roots take shape around the old fallen trunk and keep their shape long after the nurse log has disappeared. Reversed, ask yourself: Upon whose legacy have you grown? It's time to express your gratitude.

41. THE HOLLOW

Comfort, a settling into, hermitage

A hollow is a small valley between two mountain ridges, and often a place where forests are dense, animals gather, and springs flow into clear streams. Historically, these were often logical places to build a small family cabin, where all of life's necessities are to be found just outside the door. The Hollow card comes at a time when a settling down is needed; a turning inward toward the feelings, places, and people you call home.

REVERSED:

Hollows are a good place to hide for those who don't want to be found. Some seek them out to live the life of a hermit, others to escape the life they have. Are you running from something?

42. THE ANCIENT FOREST

Wisdom, safety, wholeness

Ancient old-growth forests are dense woodlands populated with trees that can be hundreds of years old. The trees are strong and healthy and protect each other and their understory from wind and extreme temperatures. With the growth cycle of the forest having reached its terminal phase, everything under the canopy thrives in a healthy and vibrant ecosystem. The Ancient Forest card finds you in a place of time-tested self-understanding and growth. Celebrate how far you've come.

REVERSED:

When an old-growth forest reaches its late stages, it's seldom that anything new is introduced to the system. Only a "reset" by wildfire will force a new cycle to begin, and so reversed, the Ancient Forest card finds you in a state of stagnation. What metaphorical wildfire must take place to allow you to grow anew?

The land knows you,
even when you are lost.

—ROBIN WALL KIMMERER

READINGS

Readings are the way that cartomancy practitioners structure the insights of their cards into a flow of information. The order in which cards are drawn leads the reader on a journey of situational reflection, providing beginning and end points for their query. Further, a group of drawn cards can contextualize and modify each other at times in a deeper alchemy. Be it a single card, or a multitude of cards, each "spread" provides a different breadth and depth of engagement to the experience.

Following is a selection of spreads that are unique to this oracle deck, and some you may find similar to traditional Tarot spreads. If you are new to cartomancy, these spreads are listed in order of complexity, and so it's suggested that you try the first before moving on. If you are a seasoned practitioner, you may feel adventurous and create new spread layouts that feel appropriate to your own internal landscape.

It's recommended you keep a journal to document your card spreads; where they take you, what they're about, and what new insights you've found along the way.

ON TRAIL

A single card for the world right under your feet

This is the simplest and most straightforward way to read *The Bloodlands Oracle*. It begins by thinking of an open-ended question that relates to something in your life that needs more clarity. It can be something as general as *"What does today have in store?"* to something as specific as *"How will I find the patience I need to finish this project?"* Shuffle the cards as many times as you need, letting your question crystallize in the forefront of your mind. Next, you can spread out the cards facedown and let your intuition guide you to one, or simply cut the deck and draw the top card. Any other method will work just as well. Once you have chosen a card, turn it faceup and note if it is right side up or reversed. Place the card in front of you.

Refer to the descriptions in this book for a deeper look into this moment. It may reaffirm where you're at, or it may present new insights you haven't considered yet.

THE CLIMB

A three-stage journey

Shuffle the deck as many times as you wish. While shuffling, bring a question to the forefront of your thoughts. This question should be rooted in the present time of your life but may be about anything in particular—from the granular to the universal—but let it pertain to the present. When you have formulated a question, cut the deck. Draw three cards from the top of the deck, placing them in front of you in order, in a rising line from left to right. Each card represents a stage of your journey, a climb to the summit of your query.

The first card on the left represents where you have come from, and how the journey started. Ask: *What does this card reveal about my past?* or *What events led me to this current issue?* This card is tasked with looking deeper into the choices and consequences related to your question that have shaped your experience.

The second card in the middle represents the situation at present. Ask: *What do I need to consider about my current state?* or *What actions must take place for change to occur?* This card is tasked with revealing deeper truths about the current moment.

The third card on the right represents what will help you reach resolution. Ask: *What will be different that I cannot understand now?* or *What will the consequences of my actions teach me?* This card is tasked with providing foresight into what may come in the wake of change.

Finally, as you look at the three cards as a set, or a triptych, see if you notice any physical or symbolic connections. Are there any recurring features or elements? Can you picture any relationships between the imagery in the cards? Do the meanings of the cards relate to each other or contrast? Is there a deeper story across them? Where is your story most bright in them? Refer to the card descriptions to follow your unique journey through the landscape.

THE ODYSSEY

A long-form adventure through the Bloodlands

Shuffle the deck as many times as you wish. While shuffling, bring a question to the forefront of your thoughts. This question should be rooted in the present time of your life, and while it may be about anything in particular—from the granular to the universal—let it pertain to the present. When you are ready, cut the deck and begin drawing cards, nine in total. Using the pictured layout, lay each card faceup in order and orientation as shown, until all nine cards are revealed. Begin with the card in spot 1.

CARD 1—THE PATH.
This card reveals deeper truths about the current moment you are in.

CARD 2—OBSTACLES.
This card reveals any issues that need your attention.

CARD 3—REASONS.
This card asks you to consider what past experiences, values, trauma, or history are influencing the present.

CARD 4—THE TRAIL BEHIND.
This card asks what recent events have had an impact on your experience or exacerbated an issue.

CARD 5—OPPORTUNITIES.
This card provides foresight into what may come.

CARD 6—THE TRAIL AHEAD.
This card reveals actions and changes that may happen next.

CARD 7—THE SELF.
This card asks how you yourself have contributed to the situation.

CARD 8—OTHERS.
This card reveals the influence of one or multiple people on the situation.

CARD 9—RESOLUTION.
This card reveals the potential endpoint of the previous influences. Not to be considered a reliable prediction, rather, this card points in a direction of where things seem to be going, on the basis of the collective interpretation of the other eight cards. It is a flexible and malleable outcome though. All the cards in The Odyssey are meant to inspire ways to aid in what you want or to change something you wish was different. Each reading will be different, each bringing new insights and mysteries to find in yourself.

Finally, as you look at the nine cards as a whole, see if you notice any physical or symbolic connections. Are there any recurring features or elements? Can you picture any relationships between the imagery in the cards? Do the meanings of the cards relate to each other or contrast? Is there an abundance of any particular elements in the cards you drew? Refer to the card descriptions to follow your unique journey through the landscape.

This is, I think, what holiness is:
the natural world, where every
moment is full
of the passion to keep moving.

—MARY OLIVER

AUTHOR'S NOTE

Thank you for your interest in *The Bloodlands Oracle*, and I hope it brings you insight and empowers you for the journey ahead. Cartomancy came to me at a time when I needed it most, and creating this deck was my way of showing gratitude for how it had helped me out of a personal darkness, out of a long night of the soul. I hope to pay forward that help and guidance to you through the imagery and symbolism within these cards.

Developing *The Bloodlands Oracle* began in the spring of 2020 as the COVID-19 pandemic turned the world upside down. During this mythological time in our history, I found myself isolated, a bit lost, and in need of some guidance from the land around me. After creating the *Nightfall Tarot* deck the year before, I wanted to turn my experience with card-based divination toward my own personal interests. The dark and fantastical charcoal landscape drawings that have become the central focus of my art practice seemed like a great place to look for metaphor. I began examining what the features of the land could mean to us and what they could tell us about our lives. Eventually, I began to envision life as a journey that one could take through those landforms that frequently appear in my artwork.

Since those journeys are now made possible in this oracle deck, I hope they help lessen the separation between ourselves and the living world. Further, I hope it gives us an opportunity to see our humanity reflected in other living things—the trees, the mountains, the rivers—and to feel the ways we all are growing, living, dying, and being reborn in this special land we call home. *The Bloodlands Oracle* was inspired by and created where I live in Vancouver, British Columbia, in the awe-inspiring, unceded, shared, and asserted territories of the Indigenous Musqueam, Squamish, and Tsleil-Waututh peoples.

ON CARTOMANCY:

Cartomancy is meant at its core to be enjoyable and challenging, for anyone at any level of experience. I invite you to create some flexible space for how you read and interpret the cards, and with the help of this guide, your understanding and depth of experience will grow over time. Finally, as the great Tarot master Rachel Pollack says, "Read the Tarot as an act of love," meaning that it's important to feel that you are connected to the process in an authentic way and willing to consider the insights that may come from consulting the original card meanings.

ON REVERSED CARDS:

Some cartomancy practitioners defer to the alternate meaning of a reversed card, and some disregard card orientation altogether. This is a flexible decision that you should make for yourself. I've included reversed meanings in this guide because Arthur Waite did in his first book on the Tarot, *The Pictorial Key to the Tarot*. Like him, I feel that there is a deeper interpretation to a card when it is revealed reversed, as the descriptions will show.

ON THE ARTWORK:

Each card was created using Kyle's Happy HB brush in Adobe Photoshop and a Wacom Cintiq monitor. Stylistically, it was my goal to mimic the contrast and texture of my charcoal drawings, but with the efficiency and ease of digital media. Conceptually, as in much of my art practice, I wanted all the images and meanings in *The Bloodlands Oracle* to be linked by the theme of darkness. For many people, darkness can be a mysterious and alluring force, a melancholy and protective space, or a place to confront fear. It takes courage to walk through the night, a bit of faith that the road will not end but arrive somewhere in the light. We put one foot in front of the other, we find encouragement in what forms it takes, and we do our best to be there for each other, and ourselves, along the way.

—**AMORY ABBOTT**